SimplyHealthful

Skillet Suppers

THE SIMPLY HEALTHFUL SERIES

Simply Healthful Skillet Suppers by Andrea Chesman
Simply Healthful Pizzas and Calzones by David Ricketts and Susan McQuillan
Simply Healthful Pasta Salads by Andrea Chesman
Simply Healthful Cakes by Donna Deane and Minnie Bernardino
Simply Healthful Fish by David Ricketts and Susan McQuillan

Simply Healthful

Skillet Suppers

Delicious New Low-Fat Recipes

By Andrea Chesman

Photography by Steven Mark Needham

CHAPTERS PUBLISHING LTD., SHELBURNE, VERMONT 05482

Published by
Chapters Publishing Ltd.
2031 Shelburne Road
Shelburne, Vermont 05482

Library of Congress Cataloguing-in-Publication Data

Chesman, Andrea
    Simply healthful skillet suppers : delicious new low-fat recipes
    by Andrea Chesman ; photography by Steven Mark Needham.
        p. cm. — (The Simply healthful series)
    Includes index.
    ISBN 1-881527-33-6 : $9.95
    1. Skillet cookery. 2. Quick and easy cookery. I. Title. II. Series.
    TX840.S55C49 1994
    641.7'7—dc20   93-45014

Trade distribution by
Firefly Books Ltd.
250 Sparks Avenue
Willowdale, Ontario
Canada M2H 2S4

Printed and bound in Canada by
Friesen Printers
Altona, Manitoba

Designed by Eugenie Seidenberg Delaney
Cover design by Susan McClellan

Contents

Introduction

SOME 20 YEARS AGO, when my sister was married, she expected to give all her bridesmaids jewelry as a thank you, but I coveted a wedding gift she planned to return to the department store—a set of cast-iron skillets. She graciously presented me with the skillets, and I'm happy to say both her marriage and my frying pans have endured.

Those frying pans have accompanied me cross-country and back. They have been used to sauté shrimp in city apartments and to fry pancakes over campfires. Now they hang over my stove in Vermont, and I use them often for quick suppers.

My favorite quick supper is a skillet supper—a one-dish meal made in a single skillet or frying pan. These dinners can be whipped together at the end of a long working day, when the kids are hungry and no one wants to be tested with exotic foods or complicated recipes. They are dishes that fill you up, and they are loaded with good-for-you grains or potatoes and plenty of vegetables. Some are vegetarian, but most use fish, red meat or fowl in small, healthful amounts.

I may make chili in a skillet and top it with a cornmeal batter and bake it in the oven. Or I may stir together a delicate risotto or pilaf with rice and seafood and diced vegetables, or I may prepare a hearty sauté of potatoes, turkey and vegetables. The combinations are endless, but one thing is certain: this is simple, honest food. And although no one would say skillet suppers are glamorous, they look just fine served right out of the pan. Add a green salad and a loaf of bread, and the meal is complete.

One of the nicest features of skillet suppers is how easily they can be adapted to the low-fat cooking methods that are slowly but surely becoming part of my cooking style. Just about everyone wants to cut fat from their diet; the problem is learning new techniques that make it possible. Where skillet suppers are concerned, however, no new techniques are necessary. I sauté my vegetables in less oil than you may be used to, and I use chicken broth to add the moisture and rich flavor that generous quantities of butter and olive oil once contributed, but other than that, there are no tricks to making delicious low-fat skillet suppers.

Skillet Sense

I CAN GET QUITE SENTIMENTAL about my skillets. For one thing, I expect them to outlast me—at least the cast-iron ones. Once a cast-iron skillet is well-seasoned, it requires little care and will last forever—with no warping, no chipped finish. I have no doubt that my skillets will be passed on to my kids, who will remember the hearty jambalayas, the saffron-scented paellas, the comforting corn-bread suppers that came from those pans.

Recently, I added a heavy-duty nonstick skillet to my *batterie de cuisine*. For years, I had avoided nonstick cookware because the pans were flimsy and the coatings were too delicate to survive more than six months' use. But today's pans come in tough, durable models that do a good job of both browning foods and standing up to steady use. I find I can use my nonstick and cast-iron skillets interchangeably, except when a recipe requires no oil; then only a nonstick skillet will do.

If you don't have a big, heavy-duty skillet—made of cast iron or with a nonstick or stick-resistant coating—you will not be able to make the recipes in this book. Nonstick skillets are metal frying pans that have been treated with silicone and polyfluorethylene, whose trade names include Tefal, Teflon and Silverstone. These space-age thermoplastic coatings resist sticking, allowing you to cook with little or no fat and facilitating clean-up. Stick-resistant cookware, such as stainless steel and enamel, requires using a little fat. These pans must also be preheated and the ingredients added slowly, or food will stick. For the recipes in this book, I greatly prefer my nonstick pans.

You'll want a heavy-duty pan that conducts heat evenly, so there are no hot spots where food may scorch. Copper and cast iron are good heat conductors. Stainless steel is often sandwiched with copper for better heat conducting. Look for a skillet with ovenproof handles so you can put it in the oven. A tight-fitting lid is essential.

The only drawback of nonstick cookware is that the pieces must be treated with care, since the coatings eventually wear off. To prolong the life of this cookware, use only plastic or wooden utensils with them. Soak in warm water to loosen any burned-on bits of food, rather than scouring. Stick-resistant cookware should be treated with the same tender care.

Cast iron also requires special treatment. A new pan must be seasoned before it is used. To do this, brush the inside of the pan with a flavorless cooking oil. Then add enough oil to measure ¼ inch deep in the pan. Heat the pan for 1 hour in a 300-degree F oven. Cool, pour off any excess oil and wipe the pan clean with a paper towel.

Some people wash their cast-iron cookware in soap and water, dry the pan, and re-season it by brushing on more oil, heating briefly, then wiping clean. However, if you do not use soap and water and simply wash the pan after use with a clean cloth, you can avoid this step. Burned-on foods can be released by scouring with salt before the pan is wiped clean. Cast iron will absorb food odors, so after cooking a strongly flavored dish like Indian curry, you may want to wash with soap and water and then re-season.

To make the recipes in this book, you will need a large skillet: my cast-iron skillet measures 10 inches around on the bottom; my nonstick skillet measures 11½ inches. This is the minimum size you will need to cook dinner for four.

Suppers of Convenience

My idea of a skillet supper is a dish that provides a complete meal. Salads and breads complement skillet suppers, but you won't need other side dishes because the suppers included here always contain vegetables. And with very few exceptions, they contain rice, grains, pasta or potatoes. (The exceptions are a couple of meat-and-vegetable combinations hearty enough to stand on their own.) All of the recipes can be prepared in less than an hour; most take 30 to 45 minutes, from start to finish.

The cooking goes quickly in these skillet recipes, so be sure you have all the ingredients chopped and ready before you turn on the heat. Indeed, you can liken most skillet recipes to stir-fry recipes: the chopping may take more time than the cooking.

Because I want these recipes to be quick, I make free use of three canned ingredients: tomatoes, beans and broth. Feel free to substitute home-cooked ingredients (use 2 cups of chopped fresh tomatoes for 15 ounces of canned chopped tomatoes and 2 cups cooked beans for 15 ounces of canned), but don't feel you are necessarily sacrificing flavoring. I use canned tomatoes because they taste better than fresh at least 10 months of the year. There are a few canned broths on the market that are comparable to homemade. Taste several brands before settling on one. I avoid those that contain hydrolyzed yeast, which I think gives soup a canned flavor. If you find a recipe requires slightly more than 1 can of broth, just add water to get the necessary yield; there is no point in opening a second can.

The recipes that follow are designed to feed four, with the occasional recipe feeding three or five, depending on how far the ingredients go without opening up a second can or using half of this or that. I prefer recipes that don't generate leftovers; half an onion or tomato is likely to spoil in my refrigerator. Because I hate cookbooks where the portions are so minuscule they could satisfy only the most abstemious, my serving sizes are generous.

Perfect Rice

PAELLA, PILAF, JAMBALAYA AND RISOTTO . . . the list of wonderful skillet rice dishes is extensive. It isn't at all difficult to cook rice well, but it does require attention to the details. I find that plain white or brown rice boiled in a saucepan is a good deal more forgiving than rice cooked in a skillet.

There are many different opinions as to how to cook rice, whether to wash the grains or not and what proportions of water work best. Depending on the type of rice you are using, various cooking methods are effective. What follows is the one I have found works best.

First, unless you are making risotto, wash the rice to remove surface debris and excess starch. This will also wash away some of the vitamins and minerals that have been sprayed onto the rice to enrich it, but that loss will be minor. Do not wash the rice for risotto; the starch on the surface of the rice contributes to the creamy texture you are trying to achieve. To wash the rice, place it in a sieve and set the sieve in a bowl of cold water. Swish the rice around until you see the water turn milky white. Drain the rice and repeat the process. Then drain the rice again. If you skip this step, the rice will be not be pleasantly dry, with each grain distinct and separate; rather, it will tend to clump together.

Next, toast the rice by tossing it with the seasonings in the skillet over medium-high heat until the grains appear dry and white; this usually takes 3 to 5 minutes. Do not let the rice scorch. Then stir in the liquid specified in the recipe (the proportion of rice to liquid is usually 1 cup rice to 2 cups liquid). Bring the mixture to a boil, reduce the heat to maintain a *gentle boil* and cover the pot. If the pot is not tightly covered, the recipe will not provide enough liquid and the rice will be slightly hard on the inside. If you cook the rice too fast, it will boil over the sides of the skillet and make a mess, but if you cook it too slowly, it will be mushy. Check the rice after 12 minutes. It is done when the liquid is all absorbed and steam holes appear on the surface. It should be firm, not sticky or gummy (which indicates overcooking). If the rice is almost but not quite done, remove it from the heat and let it sit, covered, for about 3 minutes more. Then remove the cover and fluff with a fork.

If you plan to hold the rice for more than a few minutes before serving, dry the lid to remove any condensation. Crumple a dishtowel or paper towel and place it on top of the rice before setting the lid back on the pot. This will prevent steam from condensing on the lid and falling back on the rice, making it mushy.

The heat over which you cook the rice is probably the most important factor. If you cook it over too low a flame, it will be mushy on the outside, with a hard kernel inside. A gentle boil should be maintained so that white rice is cooked in 12 to 15 minutes. Rice that is first cooked and then added to the skillet should be prepared as above, but toasting it is not necessary.

Serving Skillet Suppers

ALL OF THESE SUPPERS are meant to be cooked and eaten on the spot. You can bring the skillet to the table or serve out portions with a spoon from the kitchen. These rustic meals are colorful combinations of grains and vegetables that will appeal to everyone. And whoever does the dishes will be happy to discover that there is little cleanup afterwards.

Vegetarian Skillet Suppers

Risotto Primavera

Greet the spring with this light combination of rice and spring vegetables. Risottos are made by slowly adding broth to short-grain rice while stirring. The result is a creamy-textured rice, which sets off the tender-crisp asparagus and peas. This risotto is quite light, but the serving size is generous. It goes well with a loaf of French country bread and a salad of spring greens.

Arborio rice, imported from Italy, is perfect for making a creamy risotto, but any short-grain rice will do.

5½	cups vegetable or defatted chicken broth
½	cup white wine
1	pound asparagus, trimmed, cut into 1-inch pieces
1	teaspoon extra-virgin olive oil
1½	cups Arborio or other short-grain white rice
½	red bell pepper, diced
2-3	cloves garlic, minced
1	cup fresh or frozen peas
¼	cup freshly grated Parmesan cheese
	Salt and freshly ground black pepper to taste
6	fresh basil leaves, shredded, or 1-2 teaspoons finely minced lemon zest

1. Heat broth and wine to simmering in medium saucepan.

2. Meanwhile, blanch asparagus in water to cover for 1 minute. Drain and rinse under cool running water to stop cooking. Set aside.

3. Heat oil in large nonstick or cast-iron skillet over medium-high heat. Add rice, bell pepper and garlic and toss to coat with the oil. Sauté for about 3 to 5 minutes, until rice appears toasted.

4. Add 1 cup simmering broth mixture to rice and reduce heat to medium. Stir until the liquid is mostly absorbed. Continue adding more broth, 1 cup at a time, cooking and stirring as liquid is absorbed. It will take 18 to 25 minutes for all liquid to be absorbed; rice should have firm but creamy consistency.

5. Stir in asparagus, peas and Parmesan cheese. Add salt and pepper. Stir in basil or lemon zest. Cover and let stand for about 3 minutes to allow vegetables to heat through. Serve at once.

Makes 4 servings.

424 CALORIES PER SERVING: 19 G PROTEIN; 4 G FAT; 71 G CARBOHYDRATE; 1,192 MG SODIUM; 5 MG CHOLESTEROL.

Each bite provides the flavor of lasagna, but little work is involved in the preparation. I use flat noodles, such as farfalle, to give this mixed-up skillet version the texture of a layered lasagna, and moisten them with tomato sauce and cheese. Although spinach is popular in vegetarian lasagnas, I prefer the more robust flavor and texture of kale.

Vegetarian Skillet Lasagna

¾	pound flat pasta, such as farfalle (butterflies) or orecchiette (little ears)
2	teaspoons extra-virgin olive oil
2	cups sliced mushrooms
1	onion, diced
1	green bell pepper, diced
4	cloves garlic, minced
1	can (29 ounces) tomato sauce
2	tablespoons chopped fresh oregano or 2 teaspoons dried
1	tablespoon chopped fresh basil or 1 teaspoon dried
1	cup part-skim ricotta
2	egg whites, lightly beaten
2	tablespoons chopped fresh basil or ¼ cup chopped fresh parsley
	Salt and freshly ground black pepper to taste
4	cups chopped fresh kale
½	pound part-skim mozzarella, cubed

1. Cook pasta in boiling salted water until just done, about 7 minutes; do not overcook. It should be quite firm. Drain and set aside.

2. In large nonstick or cast-iron skillet, heat oil over medium-high heat. Add mushrooms, onion and bell pepper and sauté until limp, about 3 minutes. Add garlic and sauté 1 minute more.

3. Add tomato sauce, oregano and basil. Reduce heat and simmer for about 10 minutes.

4. While sauce simmers, combine ricotta, egg whites and basil or parsley. Set aside.

5. Taste sauce and adjust seasonings, adding salt and pepper, if necessary. Carefully stir in kale. Continue stirring until well wilted. Carefully stir in pasta, mozzarella, then ricotta mixture. Cover and simmer for 15 minutes.

6. Remove from heat and let sit uncovered for at least 10 minutes before serving.

Makes 4 to 5 servings.

705 CALORIES PER SERVING: 39 G PROTEIN; 19 G FAT; 97 G CARBOHYDRATE; 1,632 MG SODIUM; 51 MG CHOLESTEROL.

Tex-Mex Skillet Supper Corn Bread

BEAN FILLING

2	tablespoons canola or olive oil
2	teaspoons ground cumin
1	onion, finely diced
½	green bell pepper, finely diced
½	red bell pepper, finely diced
1-3	hot red or green peppers, finely diced
1	can (15 ounces) diced tomatoes, with juice
1	can (15 ounces) black beans, rinsed and drained
2	tablespoons chopped fresh cilantro (optional)
	Salt and freshly ground black pepper to taste

CORN BREAD TOPPING

1	cup yellow cornmeal
¾	cup all-purpose flour
2	tablespoons sugar
2	teaspoons baking powder
1	teaspoon salt
1	cup skim or low-fat milk
2	egg whites
2	tablespoons canola or vegetable oil

1. Preheat oven to 425 degrees F.

2. Prepare Bean Filling: Heat 2 tablespoons oil in large ovenproof nonstick or cast-iron skillet over medium-high heat. Stir in cumin. Add onion, bell peppers and hot peppers and sauté until onion is translucent, about 3 to 5 minutes. Then add tomatoes and juice, black beans and cilantro, if using. Cook for 1 minute more. Remove from heat. Season with salt and pepper.

3. Prepare Corn-Bread Topping: In medium-size bowl, combine cornmeal, flour, sugar, baking powder and salt. Mix well. Place milk in

Make this Southwest-style bean-and-corn-bread dish as spicy or as mild as you like, and pass salsa at the table. When you spread the corn-bread batter over the beans in the skillet, the recipe proportions may look wrong: there will seem to be too little batter. Don't worry; just spread out the batter as evenly as possible. As the corn bread bakes, it will rise nicely.

(continued on page 20)

large glass measuring cup. Add egg whites and oil to milk and mix well. Pour into flour mixture and stir just until moistened. Batter will be lumpy. Spread batter as evenly as possible over beans in skillet.

4. Bake for about 20 to 25 minutes, or until top is golden and firm. Let stand for about 5 minutes before serving with pie server or spoon.

Makes 4 to 5 servings.

575 CALORIES PER SERVING: 21 G PROTEIN; 16 G FAT; 90 G CARBOHYDRATE; 936 MG SODIUM; 1 MG CHOLESTEROL.

Vegetable Couscous

2	tablespoons olive oil
1	teaspoon turmeric
½	teaspoon ground ginger
½	teaspoon ground cayenne
1	medium eggplant (1 pound), peeled and diced
1	onion, diced
½	head green cabbage (1¼ pounds), diced
1	teaspoon soy sauce
2	cups vegetable or defatted chicken broth
1	can (15 ounces) diced tomatoes, with juice
1	red bell pepper, diced
1	cup raisins
2	teaspoons chili paste with garlic or more to taste
1	cup uncooked couscous
1	cup cooked chick-peas

1. In large nonstick or cast-iron skillet, heat oil over medium-high heat. Stir in turmeric, ginger and cayenne. Add eggplant and onion. Sauté until eggplant is slightly soft, about 4 minutes.

2. Add cabbage and soy sauce and continue to sauté for another 2 minutes, until cabbage is wilted. Cover and cook for 3 minutes.

3. Add broth, tomatoes and juice, bell pepper, raisins and chili paste. Bring to boil.

4. Stir in couscous, cover and reduce heat to gentle simmer. Cook for about 15 minutes, until couscous is tender, but mixture is still moist. Stir in chick-peas. Taste and adjust seasonings before serving.

Makes 4 servings.

533 CALORIES PER SERVING: 16 G PROTEIN; 9 G FAT; 101 G CARBOHYDRATE; 899 MG SODIUM; 0 MG CHOLESTEROL.

Made from ground semolina, couscous looks like tiny beads and has a delicate taste. Traditionally, it is paired with bold seasonings. This one gets its heat from Chinese chili paste with garlic, found where Asian foods are sold. Layers of flavor are added with savory vegetables, chick-peas and sweet raisins. The result is a complex dish, with multiple flavors and textures.

Two-Grain Summer Vegetable Pilaf

½	cup wild rice
2	cups uncooked couscous
1	tablespoon olive oil
1½	pounds eggplant (1 medium-large), peeled and diced
1	onion, halved lengthwise and slivered
1	green bell pepper, julienned
1	carrot, julienned
6	cloves garlic, minced
2	cups chopped tomatoes, fresh or canned
1	cup fresh or frozen peas
¼	cup chopped fresh basil
	Juice of 1 lemon
	Salt and freshly ground black pepper to taste

1. Combine wild rice and 2 cups water in small saucepan. Bring to boil, cover and reduce heat. Simmer for about 40 minutes, until rice is tender (test by biting a couple of grains) and most grains have burst open. Drain excess water. Set aside.

2. Combine couscous and 4 cups boiling water in large bowl. Cover and let steam for about 10 minutes. Fluff with fork and set aside.

3. In large nonstick skillet, heat oil over medium-high heat. Add eggplant and onion and sauté until eggplant is soft and onion begins to brown, about 5 minutes. Add bell pepper, carrot and garlic and sauté about 3 minutes more.

4. Stir in wild rice and couscous. Carefully stir in tomatoes, peas, basil, lemon juice, salt and pepper. Serve hot.

Makes 5 to 6 servings.

452 CALORIES PER SERVING: 16 G PROTEIN; 4 G FAT; 90 G CARBOHYDRATE; 27 MG SODIUM; 0 MG CHOLESTEROL.

Fine-textured couscous and chewy grains of wild rice combine in this lemon-and-basil-scented pilaf. Wild rice has a nutty, smoky flavor that perfectly complements couscous and other grains. Its expensive price tag reflects the work that is involved in its preparation for market. Although technology has transformed some wild rice areas, most grains are harvested as they have been for centuries, by Native Americans in birch canoes, with one person pushing the boat through the shallow lake with a pole while the other bends the plants down over the boat and beats out the grain. (Some grain inevitably falls back into the water, providing the seed for next year's harvest.) Then the seed is hulled to separate the grain.

Barbecued Beans Skillet Supper Corn Bread

BEAN FILLING

1	tablespoon canola or olive oil
1	teaspoon chili powder
1	small onion, diced
1	small green bell pepper, diced
1-3	hot red or green peppers, diced (optional)
1	can (15 ounces) kidney beans, rinsed and drained
⅔	cup tomato-based barbecue sauce
⅓	cup water

CORN-BREAD TOPPING

1	cup yellow cornmeal
¾	cup all-purpose flour
1	tablespoon sugar
2	teaspoons baking powder
1	teaspoon salt
1	cup skim or low-fat milk
2	egg whites
2	tablespoons canola oil
1½	cups frozen corn

1. Preheat oven to 425 degrees F.

2. Prepare Bean Filling: Heat 1 tablespoon oil in large ovenproof nonstick or cast-iron skillet over medium-high heat. Add chili powder and mix into oil. Add onion, bell pepper and hot peppers (if using), and sauté until onion is translucent, about 3 minutes. Then add beans, barbecue sauce and water. Cook for 1 minute more. Remove from heat.

3. Prepare Corn Bread Topping: In medium-size bowl, combine cornmeal, flour, sugar, baking powder and salt. Mix well. Place milk in large

glass measure. Add egg whites and oil to milk and mix well. Pour into flour mixture along with frozen corn and stir just until well moistened. Batter will be lumpy. As evenly as possible, spread batter over beans in skillet.

4. Bake for about 20 minutes, or until top is golden and firm. Let stand for about 5 minutes before serving with pie server or spoon.

Makes 4 servings.

531 CALORIES PER SERVING: 18 G PROTEIN; 13 G FAT; 89 G CARBOHYDRATE; 1,434 MG SODIUM; 1 MG CHOLESTEROL.

A basic, satisfying vegetarian dish made with pantry staples, this rice-and-bean combination is flavored with Southwestern accents of hot peppers, tomatoes, chili, cumin and cilantro.

Red Rice and Black Beans

2	cups long-grain white rice
2	tablespoons canola or olive oil
½	onion, finely chopped
½	green bell pepper, finely chopped
1-2	hot peppers, finely chopped, plus 1 hot pepper, cut in rings, for garnish (optional)
1	tablespoon chili powder
1	teaspoon ground cumin
1	can (15 ounces) diced tomatoes
½	teaspoon salt
1	can (15 ounces) black beans, drained and rinsed
¼-½	cup chopped fresh cilantro
	Salt and freshly ground black pepper to taste

1. Wash rice in at least two changes of water. Drain well. Set aside.

2. Heat oil in large nonstick or cast-iron skillet over medium-high heat. Add rice, onion, bell pepper, hot peppers (if using), chili powder and cumin. Sauté, stirring constantly, until rice appears white and toasted, 5 to 8 minutes.

3. Meanwhile, drain tomatoes, pouring juice into large glass measure. Add enough boiling water to juice to make 4 cups. Add 4 cups tomato liquid, tomatoes and salt to skillet. Stir well. Cover, bring to boil, reduce heat and gently boil until liquid is all absorbed, about 15 minutes.

4. Fluff rice with fork. Stir in black beans and cilantro. Add salt and pepper. If desired, garnish with hot pepper rings.

Makes 4 servings.

559 CALORIES PER SERVING: 16 G PROTEIN; 9 G FAT; 104 G CARBOHYDRATE; 466 MG SODIUM; 0 MG CHOLESTEROL.

Mushroom Lo Mein

Meaty shiitake mushrooms give this vegetarian combination of noodles, tofu, broccoli and Chinese flavorings a robust taste. The lo mein is flavored by oyster sauce, a condiment that is derived from oysters. Strict vegetarians may prefer to substitute hoisin sauce, a Chinese barbecue sauce that will yield a completely different—though delicious—result.

TOFU AND MARINADE

1	tablespoon soy sauce
1	tablespoon oyster sauce
1	tablespoon dry sherry
1	teaspoon sugar
2	cloves garlic, minced
1	pound tofu, diced

LO MEIN

1	cup dried shiitake mushrooms
1½	cups boiling water
1	pound Chinese egg noodles or linguine
1	tablespoon sesame oil
¼	cup oyster sauce
1	tablespoon cornstarch
1	stalk broccoli, including florets, stem julienned
1	onion, halved lengthwise and slivered
2	cloves garlic, minced
2	teaspoons soy sauce
1	cup button mushrooms, sliced
1	cup bean sprouts

1. Prepare Tofu and Marinade: In medium bowl, mix together soy sauce, oyster sauce, sherry, sugar and garlic. Add tofu, gently toss to coat and set aside.

2. Prepare Lo Mein: Combine shiitakes and water in small bowl and set aside to soak. Cook noodles according to package directions until just tender. Drain and toss with sesame oil. Set aside.

3. Slice shiitakes into narrow slivers, discarding tough stems; reserve 1 cup soaking water. Combine soaking water, ¼ cup oyster sauce and cornstarch in small bowl and set aside.

4. In large nonstick skillet (do not use cast iron) over medium-high heat, combine broccoli, onion, garlic and 2 teaspoons soy sauce. Cook, tossing constantly, until onion is limp and broccoli bright green, about 4 minutes. Transfer to bowl and keep warm.

5. Combine shiitakes with button mushrooms in large skillet and cook, tossing constantly, for about 4 minutes, until mushrooms are golden. Add tofu and marinade and bean sprouts; mix well.

6. Add noodles and oyster-sauce mixture. Toss carefully. Bring to a boil and boil until sauce thickens and is mostly absorbed, about 1 minute. Top with broccoli and onions and serve at once.

Makes 4 servings.

652 CALORIES PER SERVING: 30 G PROTEIN; 11 G FAT; 111 G CARBOHYDRATE; 1,078 MG SODIUM; 0 MG CHOLESTEROL.

Mediterranean Eggplant Sauté With White Beans

1 tablespoon extra-virgin olive oil
1½ pounds eggplant (medium or large), peeled and diced
1 onion, halved lengthwise and slivered
6 cloves garlic, minced
1 green bell pepper, diced
2 medium zucchini (1 pound), diced
2 cups defatted chicken or vegetable broth
1 can (15 ounces) diced tomatoes
¼ cup chopped fresh basil
1 can (15 ounces) cannellini (white kidney beans), drained and rinsed
1 tablespoon capers
2 tablespoons fresh lemon juice
Salt and freshly ground black pepper to taste

1. Heat oil in large nonstick skillet (do not use cast-iron) over medium-high heat. Add eggplant and onion and sauté until eggplant is soft and beginning to brown, about 5 minutes.

2. Add garlic, bell pepper and zucchini, and sauté until zucchini is tender, about 5 minutes.

3. Add broth. Cook over medium heat for about 10 minutes.

4. Add tomatoes and basil and cook over medium heat for 5 minutes.

5. Add cannellini beans, capers, lemon juice, salt and pepper. Continue simmering until heated through.

Makes 3 to 4 servings.

314 CALORIES PER SERVING: 16 G PROTEIN; 7 G FAT; 54 G CARBOHYDRATE; 1,217 MG SODIUM; 0 MG CHOLESTEROL.

Fish
and Seafood
Skillet Suppers

Seafood Paella

4	cups defatted chicken broth
¼	teaspoon crushed saffron threads
1	tablespoon extra-virgin olive oil
2	cups long-grain white rice
3	shallots, minced
3	cloves garlic, minced
1	cup fresh or frozen peas
¼	cup diced pimientos
	Salt and freshly ground black pepper to taste
¼-⅓	pound (1 fillet) monkfish, flounder, sole or other white fish, cut into bite-size pieces
½	pound shrimp, peeled and deveined
¼	pound calico or bay scallops
18	clams or mussels, well scrubbed
1	lemon, cut into wedges

1. Combine broth and saffron and set aside.

2. In large ovenproof nonstick or cast-iron skillet, heat oil over medium-high heat. Add rice, shallots and garlic and sauté until rice is toasted and dry, about 5 minutes.

3. Add broth mixture, reduce heat to maintain gentle boil, cover and cook until liquid is absorbed and rice is tender, about 15 minutes. Meanwhile, preheat oven to 350 degrees F.

4. When rice is cooked, fluff with fork. Stir in peas and pimientos. Season with salt and pepper. Place fish, shrimp, scallops and clams or mussels over rice. Cover and place in oven. Bake for 15 to 20 minutes, or until shrimp and scallops are firm and clam or mussel shells open (discard any that are unopened). Serve with lemon wedges.

Makes 4 servings.

589 CALORIES PER SERVING: 42 G PROTEIN; 6 G FAT; 87 G CARBOHYDRATE; 991 MG SODIUM; 133 MG CHOLESTEROL.

There are probably as many paella recipes in Spain as there are cooks, but all are luxuriously scented with saffron. This variation relies on seafood: monkfish, shrimp, scallops and clams. Consider the seafood used in this recipe as recommendations only; select whatever is fresh at the market, but do include some shellfish for a dramatic presentation.

Dominican Shrimp and Yellow Rice

Rice, shrimp and tomatoes are a classic combination in many different cuisines. In this pilaf from the Dominican Republic, the flavor accents come from cilantro and annatto, a seasoning that gives the rice a yellow color. You can find the brick-red seeds wherever Hispanic foods are sold; they are sometimes called achiote. Saffron can be substituted for annatto (add ¼ teaspoon to the chicken broth), but the flavor will be different.

2	cups long-grain white rice
2	tablespoons canola oil
1	tablespoon annatto seeds
1	pound large shrimp, peeled and deveined
1	onion, finely chopped
3	cloves garlic, finely chopped
4	cups defatted chicken broth
2	bay leaves
2	medium tomatoes, chopped
2	tablespoons chopped fresh cilantro
	Salt and freshly ground black pepper to taste
	Hot-pepper sauce to taste

1. Wash rice in at least two changes of water. Drain and set aside.

2. In large nonstick or cast-iron skillet, combine oil and annatto seeds. Heat over medium heat for 3 to 5 minutes to release flavor (the fresher the seeds, the briefer the cooking time needed). With slotted spoon, remove seeds and discard.

3. Add shrimp to oil. Sauté until just pink and firm, about 3 minutes. With slotted spoon, transfer shrimp to plate and keep warm. Add onion, garlic and rice to oil and sauté until onion is translucent and rice grains appear dry, 3 to 5 minutes. Stir in broth and bay leaves. Cover, bring to a boil, reduce heat to maintain gentle boil, and cook until all liquid is absorbed, about 15 minutes.

4. Remove bay leaves. Fluff rice well with fork. Stir in tomatoes, cilantro and shrimp. Taste and add salt and pepper. Pass hot-pepper sauce at the table.

Makes 4 servings.

547 CALORIES PER SERVING: 31 G PROTEIN; 9 G FAT; 82 G CARBOHYDRATE; 987 MG SODIUM; 175 MG CHOLESTEROL.

Sweet and hot peppers, along with cilantro and Canadian bacon, make this Caribbean-inspired combination of rice and shrimp a festival of flavors on the tongue. If asparagus is not in season, substitute another green vegetable, such as peas or green beans.

Shrimp Pilau

2	cups long-grain white rice
2	teaspoons olive oil
1	onion, minced
6	cloves garlic, minced
1	green bell pepper, minced
1-2	hot peppers, minced
1	ounce Canadian bacon, diced (about ⅓ cup)
2	cups defatted chicken broth
2	cups water
1	pound asparagus, cut into 1-inch pieces
1	pound shrimp, peeled and deveined
¼	cup fresh cilantro, minced
2	tablespoons diced pimientos
	Salt and freshly ground black pepper to taste

1. Wash rice in at least two changes of water. Drain and set aside.

2. Heat oil in large nonstick or cast-iron skillet over medium-high heat. Add onion, garlic, bell pepper, hot peppers and bacon. Sauté until vegetables are limp, about 3 to 5 minutes. Add rice and sauté for another 3 to 5 minutes, until rice is toasted.

3. Add broth and water. Bring to boil. Cover, reduce heat to maintain gentle boil and cook for about 15 minutes, until liquid is absorbed.

4. While rice cooks, blanch asparagus in boiling water to cover for about 1 minute. Drain and set aside.

5. When rice is cooked, fluff with fork. Stir in shrimp. Cover and cook over low heat for about 3 minutes, until shrimp is pink and firm. Stir in asparagus, cilantro and pimientos. Season with salt and pepper. Serve at once.

Makes 4 servings.

532 CALORIES PER SERVING: 34 G PROTEIN; 5 G FAT; 86 G CARBOHYDRATE; 760 MG SODIUM; 179 MG CHOLESTEROL.

Pad Thai (Thai Noodles With Shrimp and Peanuts)

Pad Thai is one of Thailand's national dishes, sure to be found on the menu of any Thai restaurant you may visit. This exotically flavored rice-noodle dish owes its sweetly pungent flavor to a variety of ingredients, including fish sauce (found where Asian products are sold), ginger, lime, peanuts and cilantro. Some versions are sweetened with tamarind, others with honey, ketchup or molasses.

You'll find rice sticks where Asian foods are sold; look for Thai jantaboon or Vietnamese banh pho.

¾	pound rice sticks (flat rice noodles, ¼ inch wide)
1¾	cups water
½	cup fish sauce
¼	cup fresh lime juice
3	tablespoons molasses
5	tablespoons sugar
½	teaspoon crushed red pepper flakes
1	tablespoon peanut oil
¾	pound shrimp, peeled and deveined
2	cloves garlic, minced
1	1-inch piece gingerroot, minced
2	eggs, lightly beaten
¼	cup chopped dry-roasted peanuts
2	cups bean sprouts
2	scallions, chopped
2	tablespoons chopped fresh cilantro
1	lime, cut into wedges

1. Soften rice sticks by soaking in cold water to cover for 30 minutes. Drain.

2. Meanwhile, make sauce by combining 1¾ cups water, fish sauce, lime juice, molasses, sugar and red pepper flakes. Set aside.

3. Heat oil in nonstick skillet over medium-high heat. Add shrimp, garlic and ginger and sauté until shrimp are pink and firm, about 3 minutes. Remove shrimp from skillet with slotted spoon and keep warm.

4. Pour eggs into skillet. When bottom of egg has set, about 15 to 30 seconds, add drained noodles and sauce and stir-fry or toss with two

(continued on page 42)

spoons until eggs are cooked through and most of liquid has been absorbed by noodles, about 5 minutes. Carefully mix in shrimp, peanuts, 1 cup bean sprouts and scallions.

5. Serve hot, garnished with remaining bean sprouts, cilantro and lime wedges.

Makes 4 servings.

615 CALORIES PER SERVING: 30 G PROTEIN; 13 G FAT; 96 G CARBOHYDRATE; 590 MG SODIUM; 244 MG CHOLESTEROL.

Shrimp and Rice Creole

2 cups long-grain white rice
1 teaspoon olive oil
2 celery stalks and leaves, diced
1 green bell pepper, diced
1 red bell pepper, diced
1-2 hot peppers, diced
½ onion, diced
4 cloves garlic, minced
2 cups shrimp broth or bottled clam juice
2 cups defatted chicken broth or water
1 teaspoon dried leaf thyme
¼ teaspoon ground white pepper
¼ teaspoon freshly ground black pepper
3 bay leaves
1 teaspoon hot-pepper sauce (or more to taste)
1 pound large shrimp, peeled and deveined
4 scallions, chopped
½ cup chopped fresh parsley
  Salt to taste

1. Wash rice in at least two changes of water. Drain and set aside.

2. In large nonstick or cast-iron skillet, heat oil over medium-high heat. Add celery, bell peppers, hot peppers and onion. Sauté for about 5 minutes, or until limp. Add garlic and rice; sauté for another 3 to 5 minutes, until rice looks slightly toasted. Add shrimp broth or clam juice and chicken broth or water, thyme, white and black pepper, bay leaves and hot-pepper sauce. Cover and bring to boil. Reduce heat to maintain gentle boil and cook for about 15 minutes, until liquid is absorbed.

3. Remove bay leaves. Fluff rice with fork. Stir in shrimp, scallions and parsley. Cover and simmer for about 5 to 7 minutes, or until shrimp are pink and firm. Add salt and more hot-pepper sauce, if desired.

Makes 4 servings.

483 CALORIES PER SERVING: 29 G PROTEIN; 3 G FAT; 82 G CARBOHYDRATE; 876 MG SODIUM; 174 MG CHOLESTEROL.

Don't be put off by the long ingredient list; this recipe is easy to prepare. The rich Louisiana-style flavor depends on the interaction of ingredients: sweet and hot peppers, onion, celery, garlic, black and white pepper and thyme. I like to use shrimp stock in this—made by simmering the shrimp shells in water to cover for about 20 minutes—but bottled clam juice will do. Likewise, chicken broth adds richness, but water can be substituted.

Saffron Risotto With Shrimp and Fennel

The licorice-flavored fennel and the shrimp provide wonderful foils for the saffron-infused rice in this classic risotto. Fennel—also called finocchio— is an odd-looking vegetable with a creamy white bulb base, celerylike stalks and feathery fronds that emerge from the center of the bulb. Look for it in the supermarket from fall through spring and select crisp bulbs with bright green fronds.

3	cups defatted chicken broth
2½	cups bottled clam juice or defatted chicken broth
¼	teaspoon crushed saffron threads
1	tablespoon extra-virgin olive oil
½	cup chopped fennel bulb
2	shallots, minced
2	cloves garlic, minced
1½	cups Arborio or other short-grain white rice
1	pound shrimp, peeled and deveined
2	tomatoes, chopped, or 1 cup canned diced tomatoes, well drained
3	tablespoons chopped fennel leaves

1. Combine broth, clam juice or chicken broth and saffron in saucepan and heat to barely simmering over low heat.

2. In large nonstick or cast-iron skillet, heat oil over medium heat. Add fennel bulb, shallots and garlic. Sauté until fennel softens, about 3 minutes. Add rice and continue to sauté until rice appears translucent, about 3 minutes.

3. Add 1 cup broth mixture to rice. Simmer, stirring frequently, until most of liquid is absorbed. Add another 1 cup broth and simmer until most of liquid is absorbed, stirring frequently. Stir in all remaining broth and cook until rice is tender and creamy, about 25 minutes.

4. Stir in shrimp, tomatoes and fennel leaves. Cover and cook over low heat until shrimp are pink and firm, about 3 minutes. Taste and adjust seasonings, adding salt or additional chopped fennel leaves, if desired.

Makes 4 servings.

437 CALORIES PER SERVING: 29 G PROTEIN; 5 G FAT; 65 G CARBOHYDRATE; 1,126 MG SODIUM; 174 MG CHOLESTEROL.

Cajun Macque Choux

A luxurious Cajun specialty of creamed corn, made rich with bacon and shrimp. The fresh tomatoes and basil give it a summery accent, while the hot pepper and white and black peppers contribute some heat.

5-6	ears corn
2	strips bacon
1	onion, diced
1	hot green pepper, diced
1	red bell pepper, diced
1	green bell pepper, diced
4	plum tomatoes, diced
½-¾	cup evaporated skim milk (depending on how milky the corn is)
2	tablespoons chopped fresh basil
2	teaspoons fresh thyme or 1 teaspoon dried leaf thyme
1-2	teaspoons sugar (optional)
¼	teaspoon ground black pepper
⅛	teaspoon ground white pepper
	Salt to taste
1	pound shrimp, peeled and deveined
2	scallions, including some green tops, chopped
2	tablespoons chopped fresh parsley

1. Cut corn kernels from cobs. You should have about 4 cups. Use dull knife to scrape cob to extract as much "milk" as possible. Set aside.

2. In large nonstick or cast-iron skillet, cook bacon until crisp. Drain bacon on paper towels. Reserve 1 tablespoon bacon fat and discard rest.

3. In reserved bacon fat, sauté onion, hot pepper and bell peppers over medium-high heat until limp, about 3 minutes.

4. Add corn, tomatoes, evaporated milk, basil and thyme. Taste and add sugar, if needed (it should be rather sweet). Add black and white pepper and salt. Cover, reduce heat to medium and simmer for 10 minutes.

5. Stir in shrimp. Replace cover and simmer until shrimp are pink and firm, about 3 minutes. Stir in scallions and parsley. Crumble bacon and mix in. Serve at once.

Makes 3 to 4 servings.

387 CALORIES PER SERVING: 36 G PROTEIN; 6 G FAT; 54 G CARBOHYDRATE; 422 MG SODIUM; 237 MG CHOLESTEROL.

Lime juice and salsa season this Southwestern-inspired combination of scallops, black beans, baby corn and zucchini. This delicious dish can be made in less than ½ hour. Serve with French bread or warmed flour tortillas.

Scallops and Black Beans

1	onion, halved lengthwise and slivered
1	green bell pepper, julienned
1	red bell pepper, julienned
1	tablespoon olive oil
1¼	pounds bay or calico scallops; or sea scallops, sliced in thirds
2	cloves garlic, minced
1	small zucchini, julienned
	Juice of ½ lime
1	can (15 ounces) black beans, drained and rinsed
1	can (15 ounces) baby corn, drained and rinsed
¼	cup salsa
	Salt and freshly ground black pepper to taste

1. Preheat oven to 500 degrees F. Combine onion and bell peppers in shallow baking dish. Toss with 2 teaspoons oil. Roast for about 20 minutes, until vegetables are browned. Set aside.

2. Heat remaining 1 teaspoon oil in large nonstick or cast-iron skillet over medium-high heat. Add scallops and garlic and sauté for about 5 minutes.

3. Add zucchini and lime juice and sauté for another 2 minutes.

4. Add black beans, baby corn, salsa and roasted peppers and onions. Continue to cook just long enough to heat through. Add salt and pepper. Serve hot. Pass extra salsa at table.

Makes 4 servings.

387 CALORIES PER SERVING: 36 G PROTEIN; 6 G FAT; 50 G CARBOHYDRATE; 585 MG SODIUM; 47 MG CHOLESTEROL.

Spanish Fish and Potato Sauté

1	pound new potatoes
⅛-¼	teaspoon crushed saffron threads
1	tablespoon extra-virgin olive oil
2	red bell peppers, cubed
1	green bell pepper, cubed
1	onion, sliced in wedges
4	cloves garlic, minced
1	can (15 ounces) diced tomatoes
1¼	pounds swordfish or other fresh fish, cut into bite-size cubes
	Salt and freshly ground black pepper to taste
	1 cup chopped fresh parsley

1. Cut potatoes into quarters or eighths depending on size; do not peel. Combine with water to cover in medium saucepan. Bring to boil; boil for about 5 minutes; drain. Set aside.

2. Toast saffron in small dry skillet over medium heat for 2 to 3 minutes. Set aside.

3. Heat oil in large nonstick or cast-iron skillet over medium-high heat. Add bell peppers, onion and garlic and sauté until peppers are browned, about 5 minutes. Add tomatoes and saffron and simmer for about 1 minute.

4. Add swordfish and potatoes to skillet. Season generously with salt and pepper, cover, and let cook until swordfish is cooked through, about 8 minutes.

5. Taste for seasoning, stir in parsley and serve immediately.

Makes 4 servings.

360 CALORIES PER SERVING: 32 G PROTEIN; 10 G FAT; 36 G CARBOHYDRATE; 152 MG SODIUM; 56 MG CHOLESTEROL.

Everyone needs at least one all-purpose, absolutely delicious fish recipe for whipping up on the spur of the moment. This one is mine. It is made with canned tomatoes, saffron, potatoes and peppers—ingredients I usually have on hand. In this version, I use swordfish, but in truth, any fish that looks good at the market, including shellfish, can be substituted; just adjust the cooking time accordingly.

Saffron-Scented Shrimp, Potatoes and Spinach

1½	pounds new potatoes
1½	cups dry white wine
2	tablespoons tomato paste
¼	teaspoon crushed saffron threads
1	tablespoon extra-virgin olive oil
8	large cloves garlic, minced
¼	teaspoon crushed red pepper flakes
1	pound shrimp, peeled and deveined
1	pound fresh spinach, trimmed and coarsely chopped
	Salt and freshly ground black pepper to taste

1. Cut potatoes into quarters or eighths depending on size; do not peel. Cover with water in medium saucepan. Bring to boil. Boil until just tender, about 5 minutes; drain. Set aside.

2. Combine wine, tomato paste and saffron. Set aside.

3. Heat oil in large nonstick or cast-iron skillet over low heat. Add garlic and red pepper flakes and sauté for about 3 minutes. Stir in wine mixture, increase heat to medium-high and bring to boil. Add potatoes and boil for about 3 minutes, or until sauce is reduced by half and potatoes are fully tender.

4. Add shrimp and simmer for 2 to 3 minutes, or until shrimp are pink and cooked through.

5. Carefully stir in spinach and cook, stirring constantly, until spinach is wilted, about 1 minute. Season with salt and pepper. Serve at once.

Makes 4 servings.

360 CALORIES PER SERVING: 25 G PROTEIN; 5 G FAT; 41 G CARBOHYDRATE; 339 MG SODIUM; 174 MG CHOLESTEROL.

When fresh spinach is in season, this tasty combination of shrimp, potatoes and spinach in a tomato-wine sauce is satisfying.

This sauté of fish and vegetables is simple and delicious. Lemon and garlic are all that is needed to highlight the bluefish. Have everything chopped and ready before you start cooking and plan to serve as soon as possible. A loaf of bread and a rustic red wine make good accompaniments. If bluefish is unavailable, substitute mackerel.

Lemony Bluefish With Potatoes and Zucchini

1½	pounds new potatoes
1	tablespoon extra-virgin olive oil
4	cloves garlic, minced
1	shallot, minced
1	pound bluefish, cut into bite-size chunks
2	medium zucchini (1 pound), quartered and sliced
	Juice of 2 lemons
½	cup chopped fresh parsley
	Salt and freshly ground black pepper to taste

1. Cut potatoes into quarters or eighths depending on size; do not peel. Combine with water to cover in medium saucepan and bring to boil. Boil for 5 minutes, until just tender.

2. Drain potatoes, return to saucepan, and toss with olive oil, garlic and shallot.

3. Heat large nonstick or cast-iron skillet over medium-high heat. Add potatoes and sauté until they are nicely browned, about 5 minutes.

4. Add bluefish and zucchini and sauté until bluefish is done, 3 to 4 minutes more.

5. Remove from heat and add lemon juice, parsley, salt and pepper. Toss well. Serve at once.

Makes 4 to 5 servings.

349 CALORIES PER SERVING: 27 G PROTEIN; 9 G FAT; 41 G CARBOHYDRATE; 82 MG SODIUM; 67 MG CHOLESTEROL.

Chicken Skillet Suppers

Arroz con Pollo (Rice With Chicken)

Arroz con pollo is a classic combination. This particular recipe, with its saffron-and-sherry-infused rice, is Cuban in inspiration. Green olives add a salty bite. This dish is quick to prepare and makes a complete meal with a green salad and bread.

2	cups long-grain white rice
2½	cups defatted chicken broth
½	cup dry sherry
¼	teaspoon crushed saffron threads
1	tablespoon extra-virgin olive oil
1	pound boneless, skinless chicken breast, cut into bite-size pieces
1	onion, diced
1	green bell pepper, diced
3	cloves garlic, minced
4	tomatoes, diced
1	cup fresh or frozen peas
10	pimiento-stuffed green olives, sliced (¼ cup)
	Salt and freshly ground black pepper to taste

1. Wash rice in at least two changes of water. Drain well. Set aside.

2. Combine chicken broth, sherry and saffron and set aside.

3. In large nonstick or cast-iron skillet over medium-high heat, heat oil. Add chicken and sauté 2 minutes. Add onion, bell pepper and garlic and continue to sauté until chicken is firm and white, not pink, and vegetables are limp, 3 to 5 minutes.

4. Add rice and sauté until rice appears toasted, about 4 minutes.

5. Stir chicken-broth mixture into rice. Bring to boil, cover, reduce heat to maintain gentle boil and cook until liquid is absorbed and rice is tender, about 15 minutes.

6. Fluff rice with fork. Stir in tomatoes, peas and olives. Season with salt and pepper. Serve at once.

Makes 4 to 5 servings.

687 CALORIES PER SERVING: 47 G PROTEIN; 10 G FAT; 93 G CARBOHYDRATE; 778 MG SODIUM; 87 MG CHOLESTEROL.

Curried Chicken and Broccoli Pilaf

2	cups long-grain white rice
1	tablespoon canola or olive oil
1	onion, finely chopped
1	½-inch piece gingerroot, minced
2	cloves garlic, minced
1	teaspoon curry powder
1	teaspoon chili powder
½	teaspoon ground cumin
½	teaspoon turmeric
⅛	teaspoon ground cardamom
⅛	teaspoon ground cinnamon
1	pound boneless, skinless chicken breasts, diced
2	cups defatted chicken broth
2	cups water
½	teaspoon salt
1	stalk broccoli, including florets, stem julienned
½	cup raisins
4	scallions, chopped

1. Wash rice in at least two changes of water. Drain and set aside.

2. In large nonstick skillet, heat oil over low heat. Add onion, ginger, garlic and dried spices and sauté for about 5 minutes, or until onion is softened.

3. Add chicken and rice, increase heat to medium and sauté for about 5 minutes, or until rice appears dry and toasted.

4. Add broth, water and salt. Bring to boil, cover and reduce heat to maintain gentle boil. Cook about 15 to 20 minutes, or until liquid is absorbed.

(continued on page 60)

5. While rice cooks, blanch broccoli in boiling water to cover for 1 minute. Drain and plunge into cold water to stop cooking. Drain well.

6. When rice is cooked, fluff with fork. Stir in broccoli, raisins and scallions. Taste and add more salt, if necessary. Serve hot.

Makes 4 servings.

654 CALORIES PER SERVING: 46 G PROTEIN; 8 G FAT; 98 G CARBOHYDRATE; 763 MG SODIUM; 87 MG CHOLESTEROL.

Paella With Chicken

2 cups long-grain white rice
¼ teaspoon crushed saffron threads
1 tablespoon extra-virgin olive oil
½ pound boneless, skinless chicken breast, cut into
    ¼-x-1-inch strips
¼ pound smoked turkey sausage, sliced ½ inch thick
1 onion, diced
½ red bell pepper, diced
4 cups defatted chicken broth
1 can (14 ounces) artichoke hearts, drained and quartered
1 cup frozen green peas
1 tomato, diced, or ¼ cup canned diced tomatoes, well drained
    Salt and freshly ground black pepper to taste

1. Wash rice in at least two changes of water. Drain well and set aside.

2. Toast saffron in dry nonstick or cast-iron skillet for 2 to 3 minutes over medium heat. Set aside.

3. Heat oil in large nonstick or cast-iron skillet over medium-high heat. Add chicken and cook until white, not pink, about 3 minutes. Remove from skillet with slotted spoon. Set aside.

4. In remaining oil in skillet, brown sausage for about 1 minute over medium-high heat. Add onion, bell pepper and rice. Sauté over medium heat, stirring constantly, for 3 to 5 minutes.

5. Return chicken to skillet, add broth and saffron, and stir well. Cover. Bring to boil, then reduce heat to maintain gentle boil and cook, covered, until all liquid is absorbed, about 15 minutes.

6. Fluff rice with fork. Carefully stir in artichoke hearts, peas and tomato. Add salt and pepper. Cook for another 3 to 4 minutes, until heated through.

Makes 4 to 5 servings.

628 CALORIES PER SERVING: 39 G PROTEIN; 9 G FAT; 97 G CARBOHYDRATE; 1187 MG SODIUM; 62 MG CHOLESTEROL.

Saffron rice with any number of combinations of seafood, chicken or rabbit meat can be enjoyed throughout Spain and southern France. This version takes its flavor from chicken and smoked turkey sausage. The yellow rice, accented with red tomatoes, peppers and green peas, makes a dazzling feast for the eyes as well as for the palate. For a special supper whipped up in less than an hour, this recipe can't be beat.

Cock-a-Leekie Skillet Potpie

CRUST
1½	cups all-purpose flour
½	teaspoon salt
5	tablespoons butter or margarine
5-7	tablespoons ice water

FILLING
1	pound potatoes, peeled and diced
¾	pound boneless, skinless chicken breast, cubed
2-3	leeks, well washed, white and tender green parts only, sliced (3 cups)
2	teaspoons vegetable oil
2	carrots, diced
1	cup frozen peas
½	cup diced red bell pepper
1¾	cups defatted chicken broth
2	tablespoons cornstarch
1-2	tablespoons chopped fresh dill
	Salt and freshly ground black pepper to taste

Chicken, leeks and fresh dill make a fragrant filling for this beautiful potpie. The generous amount of pastry dough allows for an attractive edging on the crust, as well as for cutouts placed on top. Roosters are perfect, but hearts are equally appealing.

1. Prepare Crust: Preheat oven to 425 degrees F. Combine flour and salt in mixing bowl. Cut in butter or margarine with pastry blender or two knives until mixture resembles coarse crumbs. Add 5 to 7 tablespoons ice water to moisten dough. Lightly mix together to form ball. Flatten it into a disk. Cover and refrigerate while you prepare filling.

2. Prepare Filling: Boil potatoes in salted water to cover until just tender, about 5 minutes. Drain, plunge in cold water to stop cooking, and drain again. Set aside.

3. In large ovenproof nonstick or cast-iron skillet over medium-high heat, sauté chicken and leeks in oil until chicken is white, not pink, about 5 minutes. Stir in carrots, peas, bell pepper and potatoes.

4. Place 2 tablespoons broth in small bowl. Stir in cornstarch to make thick paste. Set aside.

(continued on page 64)

5. Add remaining broth to skillet. Bring to boil. Stir in cornstarch mixture. Return to boil; cook for about 1 minute, until mixture thickens and clears. Remove from heat. Stir in 1 tablespoon dill. Taste and add salt and pepper, as well as remaining 1 tablespoon dill, if desired.

6. On lightly floured surface, roll out pastry dough to form a circle at least 2 inches bigger than skillet. Cut out circle at least 1 inch bigger than skillet. Fit pastry over filling in skillet. Turn under excess dough and flute edges. Form excess dough into ball, roll flat and use cookie cutters to make decorative cutouts. Moisten with milk and firmly attach to top crust. Cut holes in top crust for steam to escape.

7. Bake for 25 to 35 minutes, or until top crust is golden brown. Let stand for about 10 minutes before serving.

Makes 4 to 5 servings.

659 CALORIES PER SERVING: 37 G PROTEIN; 20 G FAT; 81 G CARBOHYDRATE; 873 MG SODIUM; 104 MG CHOLESTEROL.

Chicken Lo Mein

1   pound Chinese egg noodles or linguine
1   tablespoon sesame oil
1   cup defatted chicken broth
¼   cup oyster sauce
1   tablespoon cornstarch
4   cups shredded Chinese cabbage
2   carrots, julienned
¼   pound snow peas, strings removed
2   teaspoons soy sauce
½   pound boneless, skinless chicken breast, julienned
4   cloves garlic, minced
4   scallions, julienned

1. Cook noodles according to package directions and drain. Toss with sesame oil. Set aside.

2. Combine broth, oyster sauce and cornstarch in small bowl. Set aside.

3. Heat nonstick skillet (do not use cast iron)over high heat. Add cabbage, carrots, snow peas and 1 teaspoon soy sauce. Sauté until limp, about 3 minutes. Remove to bowl to keep warm.

4. Add chicken, garlic and remaining 1 teaspoon soy sauce to skillet. Sauté until chicken is firm and white, not pink, about 3 minutes.

5. Add oyster-sauce mixture to chicken and cook over high heat until sauce thickens and clears, about 1 minute. Add noodles and carefully toss until well coated. Add vegetables and scallions and toss carefully. Serve at once.

Makes 4 servings.

638 CALORIES PER SERVING: 38 G PROTEIN; 8 G FAT; 101 G CARBOHYDRATE; 732 MG SODIUM; 50 MG CHOLESTEROL.

With a nonstick skillet, it is possible to make lo mein without using a lot of oil. The flavor comes from the liberal use of oyster sauce, a slightly sweet and salty brown sauce that flavors many Chinese dishes. This dinner is also particularly fast to prepare: less than ½ hour from start to finish.

Chicken and Spinach With White Beans

1 tablespoon extra-virgin olive oil
1½ pounds boneless, skinless chicken breast, cut into
    bite-size pieces
2 celery stalks, minced
4 cloves garlic, minced
2 shallots, minced
1 can (15 ounces) diced tomatoes
1 teaspoon fresh rosemary or ½ teaspoon dried
1 tablespoon cornstarch
1 cup defatted chicken broth
1 can (15 ounces) cannellini (white kidney beans), drained
    and rinsed
1 package (12 ounces) fresh spinach, chopped
  Salt and freshly ground black pepper to taste
10 brine-cured black olives, chopped

The sunny flavors of tomatoes, rosemary and ripe olives provide a delicious backdrop to the chicken and spinach. This dish is best served as soon as it is ready; if you must prepare it ahead, make the chicken and sauce and add the spinach at the last minute. Serve with a crusty loaf of fresh bread for sopping up the sauce.

1. Heat 2 teaspoons oil in large nonstick or cast-iron skillet over medium-high heat. Add chicken and sauté until firm and white, not pink, about 3 minutes. Remove from skillet and keep warm.

2. Reduce heat to medium and add remaining 1 teaspoon oil. Add celery, garlic and shallots and sauté until limp and fragrant, about 5 minutes. Add tomatoes and rosemary and simmer 3 minutes.

3. Dissolve cornstarch in chicken broth and add to skillet. Bring to boil and cook until sauce is thickened. Add cannellini beans and chicken; heat through.

4. Just before serving, add spinach to skillet and toss until wilted, about 3 minutes. Season with salt and pepper.

5. Garnish with olives. Serve at once.

Makes 4 servings.

457 CALORIES PER SERVING: 60 G PROTEIN; 11 G FAT; 29 G CARBOHYDRATE; 746 MG SODIUM; 131 MG CHOLESTEROL.

Crisp, thyme-flavored potatoes provide the right contrast to the lemony chicken. Oven-roasting them makes them deliciously crusty with a minimum of oil and fuss.

Lemony Chicken With Artichokes and Roasted Potatoes

POTATOES

1½	pounds new potatoes
1	tablespoon extra-virgin olive oil
3	cloves garlic, minced
2	teaspoons fresh thyme leaves or 1 teaspoon dried leaf thyme
	Salt and freshly ground black pepper to taste

CHICKEN AND ARTICHOKES

1	tablespoon extra-virgin olive oil
1	pound boneless, skinless chicken breast, cut into bite-size pieces
	Salt and freshly ground black pepper to taste
2	cans (14 ounces each) quartered artichoke hearts, drained
½	cup defatted chicken broth
2	tablespoons fresh lemon juice
¼	cup chopped fresh parsley
¼	cup chopped black olives

1. Prepare Potatoes: Preheat oven to 425 degrees F. Cut potatoes into quarters or eighths, depending on size. Combine potatoes, oil, garlic, thyme, salt and pepper in bowl. Toss well. Spray baking sheet with vegetable-oil cooking spray. Spread out potatoes in single layer. Roast for 25 minutes. Set aside.

2. Prepare Chicken and Artichokes: In large nonstick or cast-iron skillet, heat oil over medium-high heat. Add chicken and sauté until white, not pink, 6 to 8 minutes. Season with salt and pepper.

3. Add artichokes, chicken broth and lemon juice to skillet. Cook until liquid in pan reduces and is slightly thickened, about 2 minutes.

4. Mix in potatoes. Garnish with parsley and olives. Serve at once.

Makes 4 servings.

495 CALORIES PER SERVING: 43 G PROTEIN; 13 G FAT; 57 G CARBOHYDRATE; 402 MG SODIUM; 87 MG CHOLESTEROL.

Turkey Skillet Suppers

Corn Risotto With Smoked Turkey

1	cup water
2	cups fresh or frozen corn kernels
4	cups defatted chicken broth
1	tablespoon sugar (optional; needed only if corn is frozen or not recently harvested)
½	teaspoon turmeric
1	tablespoon butter
2	cups Arborio or other short-grain rice
1	red bell pepper, diced
2	shallots, minced
¼	pound smoked turkey breast, diced
1	cup fresh or frozen peas
	Salt to taste

1. Bring water to boil. Add corn and cook, covered, for 2 minutes. Pour into blender and puree.

2. Return pureed corn to saucepan. Add chicken broth, sugar (if using) and turmeric. Heat to boiling. Reduce heat but keep mixture simmering.

3. Melt butter in large nonstick or cast-iron skillet. Add rice, bell pepper and shallots and cook over medium heat until rice looks dry, about 5 minutes.

4. Add 1 cup broth-corn mixture and cook over medium heat, stirring constantly until liquid is absorbed. Continue adding broth mixture, 1 cup at a time, cooking and stirring after each addition; liquid should be mostly absorbed before adding next cup.

5. When all broth has been added, remove from heat. Stir in turkey, peas and salt. Cover for about 2 minutes to heat peas through, then serve.

Makes 4 servings.

554 CALORIES PER SERVING: 25 G PROTEIN; 4 G FAT; 104 G CARBOHYDRATE; 828 MG SODIUM; 31 MG CHOLESTEROL.

Turkey Jambalaya

2   cups long-grain white rice
2   slices bacon
½   pound okra, sliced ¼ inch thick
1   green bell pepper, diced
1   onion, diced
3   cloves garlic, minced
4   cups defatted chicken broth
1   can (15 ounces) diced tomatoes, with juice
2   dashes hot-pepper sauce or more to taste
¼   pound smoked turkey breast, diced
¼   cup chopped fresh parsley
    Salt and freshly ground black pepper to taste

1. Wash rice in at least two changes of water. Drain and set aside.

2. In large nonstick or cast-iron skillet, cook bacon until crisp. Remove bacon and set aside on paper towels. Reserve 1 tablespoon bacon fat and discard rest.

3. In reserved bacon fat in skillet over medium-high heat, sauté okra, bell pepper, onion and garlic for 3 to 4 minutes, or until limp.

4. Add rice to skillet and continue to sauté until rice is toasted, for another 3 to 5 minutes. Stir in chicken broth, tomatoes with their juice and hot-pepper sauce. Cover and bring to boil. Reduce heat to maintain gentle boil and continue to cook until liquid is absorbed, about 15 minutes.

5. Fluff rice with fork. Mix in smoked turkey, parsley and crumbled bacon. Season with salt and pepper. Serve hot.

Makes 4 to 5 servings.

487 CALORIES PER SERVING: 24 G PROTEIN; 3 G FAT; 89 G CARBOHYDRATE; 1,025 MG SODIUM; 26 MG CHOLESTEROL.

Two popularly told stories explain how this Cajun dish got its name. The most repeated holds that the name derives from the French word for ham—jambon—most recipes for jambalaya require ham. A more colorful version of the tale describes a gentleman arriving late and hungry at a Louisiana inn. He orders the innkeeper, a man by the name of Jean, to balayez, the French word for "mix together." The innkeeper combines rice, meats and vegetables, and the guest proclaims the dish delicious, calling it, "Jean Balayez."

I like to think the latter story is true. It gives one the license to mix together just about any combination of rice, meats and vegetables. For this dish, I use bacon, smoked turkey, tomatoes, peppers and okra. If okra doesn't appeal, substitute peas, added after the rice is cooked. Pass hot-pepper sauce at the table.

Skillet Lasagna

14-16	ounces flat pasta, such as farfalle (butterflies) or orecchiette (little ears)
¾	pound Italian-style turkey sausage (sweet or hot), casings removed, or ground turkey
1	onion, finely chopped
1	green bell pepper, finely chopped
1	medium zucchini, diced
4	cloves garlic, minced
1	can (29 ounces) tomato sauce
4	teaspoons dried oregano
1	teaspoon dried basil
½	teaspoon dried leaf thyme
	Salt and freshly ground black pepper to taste
1	cup part-skim ricotta cheese
2	ounces part-skim mozzarella, grated (½ cup)
¼	cup freshly grated Parmesan cheese
¼	cup chopped fresh parsley
2	egg whites, lightly beaten
¼	teaspoon freshly ground black pepper

1. Cook pasta in boiling salted water until just done; do not overcook. Pasta should be quite firm. Drain and set aside.

2. In large nonstick or cast-iron skillet over medium-high heat, brown sausage or ground turkey for about 3 minutes. Add onion and bell pepper and sauté about 3 more minutes. Add zucchini and garlic and sauté for another minute. Drain excess fat or blot dry with paper towels.

3. Stir in tomato sauce and herbs. Season with salt and pepper. Simmer for 10 minutes. Stir again and adjust seasonings.

4. Meanwhile, mix together ricotta, mozzarella, Parmesan, parsley, egg whites and pepper in medium bowl.

5. Stir pasta and ricotta mixture into skillet. Cover and simmer for 15 minutes, stirring occasionally. Let stand about 5 minutes before serving.

Makes 5 servings.

613 CALORIES PER SERVING: 37 G PROTEIN; 14 G FAT; 85 G CARBOHYDRATE; 1,801 MG SODIUM; 69 MG CHOLESTEROL.

Each bite in this quick-to-prepare, mixed-up skillet version of lasagna provides the flavors of pasta, meat, tomato sauce and cheese. Because this is so good, and leftovers are so delicious, I cram quite a lot of pasta into the skillet. However, if you don't mind leaving a little pasta in the box, just 14 ounces will make slightly less, with fewer spills on the stovetop.

Skillet Choucroute Garni

1½   pounds red potatoes, sliced 1½ inches thick
½   pound smoked turkey sausage, sliced
1   onion, thinly sliced
2   cups defatted chicken broth
1½   pounds sauerkraut, drained and rinsed
½   pound smoked turkey breast, cut into ½-inch cubes
4   carrots, sliced ½ inch thick
3   bay leaves
½   teaspoon black peppercorns

1. In medium saucepan, cover potatoes with salted water and bring to boil. Let boil for about 1 minute, then drain.

2. In large nonstick (not cast-iron) skillet, combine turkey sausage and onion over medium-high heat. Sauté until sausage is no longer pink.

3. Add broth, sauerkraut, smoked turkey breast, carrots, bay leaves, peppercorns and potatoes. Skillet will be quite full; stir carefully. Bring to boil, then reduce heat, cover and simmer for about 20 minutes, until carrots and potatoes are tender.

4. Remove bay leaves and let stand for about 5 minutes before serving.

Makes 4 generous servings.

401 CALORIES PER SERVING: 35 G PROTEIN; 5 G FAT; 54 G CARBOHYDRATE; 1,504 MG SODIUM; 83 MG CHOLESTEROL.

Choucroute *is the French word for sauerkraut. In a traditional choucroute garni, the sauerkraut is flavored with goose fat, onions, juniper berries and white wine and served with potatoes and a variety of meats, including goose, pork and ham. This skillet version omits not only the goose fat but also the juniper berries, which are usually found only in specialty food stores. Low-fat turkey sausage and smoked turkey breast replace the traditional fatty meats. All you need to serve with this substantial meal is a loaf of hearty rye or pumpernickel bread.*

Nutrition-packed kale and beans combine with boldly flavored Italian sausage and garlicky potatoes. Serve with beer and rye bread.

Sausage and Kale With Garlic-Roasted Potatoes

1½	pounds red potatoes
1	tablespoon extra-virgin olive oil
3	cloves garlic, minced
1	teaspoon dried oregano
½	pound sweet or hot Italian turkey sausage, sliced 1 inch thick
1	onion, halved lengthwise and slivered
8	cups chopped fresh kale
1½	cups defatted chicken broth
1	can (15 ounces) cannellini (white kidney beans), drained and rinsed
	Salt and freshly ground black pepper to taste

1. Preheat oven to 425 degrees F. Spray baking sheet with vegetable-oil cooking spray. Cut potatoes into quarters or eighths, depending on size. Toss with oil, garlic and oregano in medium bowl. Spread out in single layer on baking sheet and roast for about 25 minutes, or until browned and tender.

2. Heat nonstick skillet over medium-high heat. Add sausage and onion and sauté until sausage is mostly browned, 3 to 4 minutes.

3. Stir in half kale and all chicken broth. Cook, stirring, until kale is wilted. Add remaining kale. Cover and simmer for about 5 minutes, until kale is wilted but still bright green.

4. Mix in cannellini beans, then potatoes. Season with salt and pepper. Serve at once.

Makes 4 servings.

539 CALORIES PER SERVING: 24 G PROTEIN; 22 G FAT; 62 G CARBOHYDRATE; 1,365 MG SODIUM; 47 MG CHOLESTEROL.

Turkey With Winter Vegetables

2   medium potatoes, peeled and cubed
1   rutabaga, peeled and cubed
2   teaspoons olive oil
¾   pound boneless, skinless turkey thigh, cut into cubes
2   leeks, well washed, white and tender green parts only, sliced
2   carrots, cubed
2   cloves garlic, minced
2   cups defatted chicken broth
1   teaspoon fresh thyme or ½ teaspoon dried leaf thyme
1½   tablespoons cornstarch dissolved in ¼ cup water
     Salt and freshly ground black pepper to taste
¼   cup chopped fresh parsley

1. Combine potatoes and rutabaga in saucepan with water to cover. Cover and bring to boil. Boil for 3 to 5 minutes, until tender. Drain and set aside.

2. In large nonstick or cast-iron skillet, heat oil over medium-high heat. Add turkey and sauté for 2 minutes. Add leeks, carrots and garlic and sauté for about 3 minutes.

3. Add potatoes, rutabaga, broth and thyme. Simmer for 5 minutes.

4. Add cornstarch mixture and simmer for 5 minutes more, or until turkey is cooked through and sauce is thickened. Season with salt and pepper. Sprinkle with parsley and serve.

Makes 4 servings.

349 CALORIES PER SERVING: 30 G PROTEIN; 9 G FAT; 36 G CARBOHYDRATE; 499 MG SODIUM; 73 MG CHOLESTEROL.

A delicious feast of aromatic vegetables. Be sure to serve with a loaf of French bread to mop up the tasty sauce.

Turkey and Summer Vegetable Sauté

½ pound green beans, trimmed, cut into 1-inch pieces
1 tablespoon extra-virgin olive oil
1 pound turkey breast, cut into bite-size pieces
6 cloves garlic, minced
4 tomatoes, diced
1 yellow squash, diced
1 tablespoon chopped fresh herbs (basil, oregano, thyme or any combination)
1 tablespoon capers
2 tablespoons fresh lemon juice or to taste
Salt and freshly ground black pepper to taste

1. Immerse and cook green beans in boiling water to cover for 1 minute. Plunge into cold water to stop cooking. Drain well and set aside.

2. In large nonstick or cast-iron skillet, heat oil over medium-high heat. Add turkey and garlic and sauté for about 5 minutes, until turkey is white inside and slightly browned outside.

3. Add beans and sauté for 1 minute. Add tomatoes and squash and sauté for 2 to 3 minutes, or until squash is tender.

4. Mix in herbs, capers and lemon juice. Season generously with salt and pepper. Serve hot.

Makes 4 servings.

249 CALORIES PER SERVING: 37 G PROTEIN; 5 G FAT; 15 G CARBOHYDRATE; 117 MG SODIUM; 94 MG CHOLESTEROL.

When the garden starts producing its summer bounty, we enjoy combinations of vegetables seasoned with lemon juice, capers and herbs—sometimes with turkey, sometimes with chicken or fish. The mixture of green beans, summer squash and tomatoes is a favorite, but earlier in the season, it might be sugar-snap peas, asparagus and baby carrots. Substitute whatever vegetables are ripe in the garden or available at a farmstand.

This is delicious served by itself, although sometimes, for dining al fresco, I hollow out a loaf of Italian bread and fill it with the sauté to serve as sandwiches. Or I'll double the amount of tomatoes and serve the sauté as a pasta topping.

Shepherd's Pie

Shepherd's pie is one of those homey dishes that ranks high on many people's lists of favorite foods. Topped with buttermilk mashed potatoes, this version uses low-fat ground turkey and tucks in plenty of zucchini, leeks, carrots and corn. Who would have guessed that a classic dish like this could be made with so little fat and still be ready to eat in about half an hour?

1½	pounds potatoes, peeled and sliced
1	teaspoon olive oil
1	pound ground turkey
1	leek, well washed, white and tender green parts only, sliced
1	carrot, diced
1	medium zucchini, diced
3	cloves garlic, minced
1	cup frozen corn kernels
1	cup defatted beef broth
1	tablespoon tomato paste
1	tablespoon cornstarch
½	teaspoon dried rosemary
½	teaspoon dried leaf thyme
	Salt and freshly ground black pepper to taste
1	cup buttermilk
1	teaspoon butter
	Salt and white pepper to taste

1. Bring potatoes to boil in salted water to cover. Boil until tender, about 10 minutes. Drain and set aside.

2. Meanwhile, in large ovenproof nonstick or cast-iron skillet, heat oil over medium-high heat. Add turkey and sauté for about 5 minutes, until turkey is mostly browned. Add leek and carrot and sauté for 2 to 3 minutes, until leek is limp. Add zucchini and garlic and sauté for another minute. Stir in corn and reduce heat to low.

3. In small bowl, combine beef broth, tomato paste, cornstarch and herbs. Mix well. Stir into skillet. Increase heat to medium-high and cook, stirring frequently, until mixture thickens, 1 to 2 minutes. Cook for another minute, then remove from heat. Season with salt and pepper.

4. Preheat broiler.

(continued on page 82)

5. Mash potatoes in medium bowl. Whip in buttermilk and butter. Add salt and white pepper.

6. Spoon mashed potatoes over turkey mixture in skillet, smoothing top. Place under broiler and broil until browned on top, 5 to 8 minutes. Let stand for 5 minutes before serving.

Makes 4 to 5 servings.

416 CALORIES PER SERVING: 24 G PROTEIN; 12 G FAT; 56 G CARBOHYDRATE; 379 MG SODIUM; 44 MG CHOLESTEROL.

Turkey Tamale Pie

Fragrant, cumin-scented chili and corn-rich corn bread combine in one skillet. This is a fairly mild dish—jazz it up with more chili powder or hot peppers, if you prefer.

CHILI FILLING

1	pound ground turkey
1	onion, diced
1	green bell pepper, diced
1	tablespoon chili powder
1	teaspoon ground cumin
1	can (15 ounces) tomato sauce
1	can (15 ounces) kidney beans, rinsed and drained
	Salt, freshly ground black pepper and cayenne pepper to taste
¼	pound Monterey Jack cheese, shredded (1 cup)

CORNMEAL TOPPING

2	cups fresh or frozen corn kernels
1	cup buttermilk
2	egg whites
1	cup yellow cornmeal
¾	cup all-purpose flour
3	tablespoons sugar
2	teaspoons baking powder
1	teaspoon salt

1. Preheat oven to 425 degrees F.

2. Prepare Chili Filling: Heat large ovenproof nonstick or cast-iron skillet over medium-high heat. Add turkey, onion, bell pepper, chili powder and cumin. Sauté until turkey is browned, about 5 minutes. Drain off liquid.

3. Add tomato sauce and beans. Taste and adjust seasonings, adding salt and pepper as needed, as well as additional chili powder or cayenne.

4. Spread cheese over chili.

5. Prepare Cornmeal Topping: In blender, combine corn and buttermilk and process until fairly smooth. Blend in egg whites.

(continued on page 84)

6. In medium bowl, combine cornmeal, flour, sugar, baking powder and salt. Mix well. Pour in buttermilk mixture and stir just until well moistened. Spread batter over chili mixture in skillet.

7. Bake for 20 to 30 minutes, until topping is golden and firm. (Batter with frozen corn will take longer to bake than batter with fresh corn.) Let stand for about 5 minutes before serving with pie server or spoon.

Makes 4 servings.

737 CALORIES PER SERVING: 41 G PROTEIN; 19 G FAT; 103 G CARBOHYDRATE; 1963 MG SODIUM; 70 MG CHOLESTEROL.

Beef, Pork and Lamb Skillet Suppers

Chinese Pan-Fried Noodles With Beef and Vegetables

When you are tired of simple stir-fries served with rice, try this mixture of beef, mushrooms and vegetables atop a golden noodle cake.

½	pound Asian egg noodles (Chinese *dan mian* or Japanese *ramen*) or vermicelli
2	egg whites, lightly beaten
1	tablespoon sesame oil
1	cup dried shiitake mushrooms
1½	cups hot water
1	stalk broccoli, including florets, stem julienned
¼	cup oyster sauce
2	tablespoons sherry
1	tablespoon soy sauce
1	tablespoon cornstarch
¾	pound sirloin steak or other lean beef, cut into 1½-inch strips
1½	cups sliced button mushrooms
4	cloves garlic, minced
1	1-inch piece gingerroot, peeled and minced
1	carrot, julienned
¼	pound snow peas, strings removed
1	cup bean sprouts
4	scallions, slivered

1. Cook noodles in large pot of boiling salted water until just done, 3 to 5 minutes. Drain well. Combine in bowl with egg whites. Brush 1 teaspoon sesame oil in 9-inch round cake pan. Place noodle mixture in greased cake pan. Place plate weighted with heavy object on top of noodle mixture. Set aside.

2. Combine shiitake mushrooms with hot water and set aside to soak.

3. Steam broccoli for 1 minute. Refresh in cold water. Drain and set aside.

4. Preheat oven to 200 degrees F. Remove shiitakes from soaking water and slice; reserve 1 cup soaking water. Make sauce by combining 1 cup soaking water, oyster sauce, sherry, soy sauce and cornstarch in small bowl. Set aside.

(continued on page 88)

5. To pan-fry noodle cake, lightly coat large nonstick (not cast-iron) skillet with 1 teaspoon sesame oil, using paper towel or brush to spread oil. Invert noodle cake into skillet; you may need to use spatulas to loosen noodle cake from cake pan. It should come out of pan in one cake. Cook over medium-high heat until bottom of cake is golden brown, 3 to 4 minutes. Flip and brown second side, about 2 minutes. Slide onto oven-proof plate and keep warm in oven.

6. Heat remaining 1 teaspoon sesame oil in skillet. Add beef, shiitake and button mushrooms, garlic and ginger and stir-fry for about 2 minutes, until beef is mostly done. Remove to bowl and keep warm.

7. Add broccoli, carrot and snow peas to skillet and stir-fry until vegetables are just tender-crisp, about 2 minutes.

8. Return beef-mushroom mixture to skillet. Pour in sauce, stirring constantly, and cook until sauce thickens and clears, about 2 minutes. Stir in bean sprouts and scallions and remove from heat.

9. To serve, cut noodle cake into wedges and spoon beef and vegetables over each portion.

Makes 4 servings.

507 CALORIES PER SERVING: 34 G PROTEIN; 13 G FAT; 63 G CARBOHYDRATE; 428 MG SODIUM; 58 MG CHOLESTEROL.

Lamb and Barley With Winter Vegetables

2	tablespoons olive oil
1	pound lamb (from leg), cut into bite-size pieces
1½	teaspoons dried leaf thyme
3	leeks, well washed, white and tender green parts only, sliced
1	carrot, diced
1	turnip, peeled and diced
1	red bell pepper, diced
1½	cups pearl barley
3	cups boiling water
1	teaspoon salt

1. In large nonstick or cast-iron skillet, heat oil over medium-high heat. Sprinkle lamb with 1 teaspoon thyme and sauté until well browned, about 5 minutes. Remove lamb with slotted spoon and set aside.

2. Add vegetables to skillet and sauté for about 3 minutes. Add barley and sauté for additional minute. Add boiling water, salt, remaining ½ teaspoon thyme and lamb. Stir well. Cover, reduce heat and simmer until liquid is absorbed, about 45 minutes. Fluff with fork before serving.

Makes 4 servings.

527 CALORIES PER SERVING: 28 G PROTEIN; 13 G FAT; 77 G CARBOHYDRATE; 634 MG SODIUM; 57 MG CHOLESTEROL.

Flavorful lamb and nutty barley make a great pair. The addition of aromatic leeks, turnips, carrots and bell peppers turns this rustic combination into a satisfying dish. Because barley cooks slowly, this dish takes a little over an hour to prepare. But during the 45 minutes that the barley is cooking, the pot needn't be tended.

Sautéed Pork and Peppers With White Beans

2	teaspoons olive oil
¾	pound pork tenderloin, cut into ¼-x-1-inch strips
1½	teaspoons ground cumin
1	onion, halved lengthwise and slivered
1	large green bell pepper, julienned
1	large red bell pepper, julienned
1	medium zucchini, julienned
2	cloves garlic, minced
1	can (15 ounces) cannellini (white kidney beans), drained and rinsed
1	can (15 ounces) diced tomatoes
1	can (4 ounces) chopped green chilies, drained
	Salt and freshly ground black pepper to taste
¼	cup chopped fresh parsley
2	scallions, chopped

1. In large nonstick or cast-iron skillet, heat oil over medium-high heat. Add pork and cumin and sauté for about 3 to 4 minutes, until pork is browned.

2. Add onion and bell peppers and sauté for another 2 minutes. Add zucchini and garlic and sauté until zucchini is just heated through, about 1 minute.

3. Reduce heat to low and add cannellini beans, tomatoes and chilies. Simmer for 5 minutes.

4. Add salt and pepper. Stir in parsley and scallions. Serve at once.

Makes 4 servings.

274 CALORIES PER SERVING: 27 G PROTEIN; 7 G FAT; 28 G CARBOHYDRATE; 937 MG SODIUM; 60 MG CHOLESTEROL.

Lamb Couscous

ouscous is a staple in the cooking of North Africa. The exotic blend of seasonings, lamb, vegetables and couscous should satisfy any kitchen-chair traveler you serve. Traditionally, couscous is paired with bold seasonings. Be sure to pass hot sauce at the table.

2   tablespoons olive oil
2   teaspoons ground cumin
½   teaspoon ground cinnamon
½   teaspoon chili powder
1   pound lamb (from leg), cut into bite-size pieces
1   onion, halved lengthwise and slivered
1   green bell pepper, diced
1   red bell pepper, diced
1   carrot, diced
1   medium zucchini, diced
1   can (15 ounces) diced tomatoes, with juice
2   cups defatted chicken broth
1   cup uncooked couscous
     Salt to taste

1. In large nonstick or cast-iron skillet, heat oil over medium-high heat. Stir in spices, lamb and onion. Sauté until onion is limp, about 3 minutes.

2. Add bell peppers, carrot and zucchini and continue to sauté for another 3 minutes, until lamb is mostly browned and vegetables are slightly softened.

3. Add tomatoes and juice, then broth. Stir in couscous, cover and reduce heat to gentle simmer. Cook for about 15 minutes, until couscous is tender. Mixture will still be moist. Season with salt and serve at once.

Makes 4 servings.

437 CALORIES PER SERVING: 29 G PROTEIN; 13 G FAT; 50 G CARBOHYDRATE; 460 MG SODIUM; 57 MG CHOLESTEROL.

Index